Math Intersections

A Look at Key Mathematical Concepts
Grades 6–9

■ ■

David J. Glatzer

Joyce Glatzer

DALE SEYMOUR PUBLICATIONS

Editor: Virginia Slachman
Cover design: Rachel Gage
Art for blackline masters: David Woods

Order number DS01028
ISBN 0-86651-505-4

DALE
SEYMOUR
PUBLICATIONS
P.O. BOX 10888
PALO ALTO, CA 94303

8 9 10 11-MA-02 01 00 99

Contents

Introduction

Purpose

The purpose of the blackline masters in *Math Intersections: A Look at Key Mathematical Concepts* is to offer mathematics teachers a variety of nonroutine problem activities. These student worksheets are designed to encourage critical thinking about concepts from the mathematics curriculum. The activities ask students to verbalize understandings and to contrast major mathematical ideas. The activities are intended for grades 6–9. However, each activity may be adapted to other grades. This book is a sequel to *Math Connections* by the same authors, Dale Seymour Publications, 1989. However, each book may be used independently of the other.

Philosophy

Asking questions is the chief measure used by classroom teachers to monitor and assess student learning. The authors of this program feel strongly that teachers need to go beyond simple recall and comprehension questions in order to help students solidify understanding and transfer concepts. As a result, the nonroutine problem activities in this book address higher levels of thinking, promote understanding through written expression, and encourage discussion and answer formulation through small group work in the classroom. As students use the activities in this book, they will begin functioning at higher levels of thinking and will increase their confidence regarding the ability to verbalize information about concepts. They will see mathematics as much more than a series of numerical answers.

Organization

The book is organized in six sections, each with a different activity format. Each section contains problems from several content categories, such as fractions, decimals, percents, number theory, geometry, measurement, and pre-algebra. The problems are arranged in order of difficulty. Note that many of *Math Intersections'* concepts are repeated in different sections of the book in different formats. This repetition facilitates mastery.

Each section contains an introduction that explains the nature of the section's activity, provides a work-through of sample problems, and describes the section's follow-up problems. Each page concludes with a follow-up activity called *STOP . . . AND THINK*. These questions are intended to help you assess the students' overall understanding and help them reach closure.

Suggested answers are provided in the Answer Section of this book, though, for many problems, students may come up with other acceptable solutions or rationales. As a model, the first problem on each page is answered for the student.

Use of the Material

There is no one way to use this book. It can be adapted to the needs of your students. However, they will receive the greatest benefit if you provide opportunities for them to share the thought processes they used in arriving at their answers.

- Classroom discussion—Make a photocopy of the page for each student and a transparency of the same page for yourself. Discuss the problems one at a time, encouraging the students to support their answers. You may decide to only use one or two questions for warm-up purposes at the start of a class period.

- Small-group work—Divide the students into small groups (of, say, three or four each), and have each group thoroughly discuss each problem. This approach may follow the model of cooperative learning groups.

- Share with a neighbor—Ask the students to complete the page independently and then share their responses with a partner.

- Student-generated extensions—When the class finishes a page, ask the students to write additional problems of the same form. (For an example, see follow-up problems for "Dictionary Revisited.")

Conclusion

Remember that the activities in this book:

- Can be used at any time of the year
- Can be used to provide variety in the math curriculum
- Can be used to preview and review
- Can be used to increase student involvement
- Are easily adaptable
- Are open-ended and easily extended
- Are fun

The ideas contained in this book have been used successfully in classrooms at the middle and secondary levels.

Section 1
Three vs. One

Introduction

The *Three vs. One* activity allows students to concentrate on the critical attributes of specific mathematical topics. This activity is more comprehensive than a consideration of opposites; students are asked to provide three examples that satisfy a given condition and one that does not. Each exercise focuses on a definition or a relationship. If the student is able to successfully complete the exercise, the implication is that he/she understands the definition or relations being explored. Hence, this activity provides an important alternative to asking recall questions that address definitions. The directions are open-ended so students are bound to provide different examples. The variety of responses should be shared with the entire group.

SAMPLE EXERCISES

For each problem, provide three examples that satisfy the given condition and one that does not.

Example 1:

	Condition	Three	One
1.	**Write four numbers:** three that are odd numbers and one that is not.	3, 5, 9	2

The terminology "one that is not" allows for the fourth number to possess characteristics other than simply even. Fractions or decimals satisfy the not-odd criteria. As a result, another possible response might be 3, 5, 9, 2.5.

Example 2:

	Condition	Three	One
1.	**Write four angle measures:** three that are measures of acute angles and one that is not.	30°, 45°, 89°	100°

The fourth angle provided could be right, obtuse, or an angle of measure greater than or equal to 180°.

To assess the student's understanding of this activity, the followup problem on each page asks the student to select one odd item from among four similar ones. The student's selection should be based on an analysis of the characteristics of the items. With these open-ended directions, different responses may result. For instance, in the *STOP . . . AND THINK* problem for "Number Theory," students are asked to select the "oddball" among 27, 63, 91, 81. One possible response is 91, because the other three numbers are divisible by 9 and 91 is not.

Number Theory

For each problem, provide three examples that satisfy the given condition and one that does not.

	Condition	Three	One
1.	**Write four whole numbers:** three that are prime and one that is not.	2, 3, 7	12
2.	**Write four whole numbers:** three that are factors of 36 and one that is not.		
3.	**Write four whole numbers:** three that are multiples of 6 and one that is not.		
4.	**Write four three-digit numbers:** three that are divisible by 3 and one that is not.		
5.	**Write four whole numbers:** three that are perfect squares and one that is not.		
6.	**Write four whole numbers:** three that are perfect cubes and one that is not.		
7.	**Write four numbers:** three that are in scientific notation and one that is not.		
8.	**Write four pairs of numbers:** three that have an average of 25 and one that does not.		

■ ■

. . . AND THINK

Examine the following set of numbers. Select one of the numbers that does not belong with the other three and state the reason for your selection.

27   63   91   81

Fractions

For each problem, provide three examples that satisfy the given condition and one that does not.

	Condition	Three	One
1.	**Write four fractions:** three that are less than $\frac{1}{2}$ and one that is not.	$\frac{1}{3}, \frac{1}{4}, \frac{1}{5}$	$\frac{2}{3}$
2.	**Write four fractions:** three that are equivalent to $\frac{3}{8}$ and one that is not.		
3.	**Write four fractions:** three that are greater than $\frac{1}{2}$ and one that is not.		
4.	**Write four fractions:** three that are improper and one that is not.		
5.	**Write four fractions:** three that have terminating decimal forms and one that does not.		
6.	**Write four fractions:** three that are between $\frac{1}{2}$ and $\frac{3}{4}$ and one that is not.		
7.	**Write four pairs of fractions:** three pairs whose sum equals 1 and one pair that does not.		
8.	**Write four pairs of fractions:** three that have a product of 1 and one that does not.		

- -

. . . AND THINK

Examine the following set of fractions. Select one of the fractions that does not belong with the other three and state the reason for your selection.

$$\frac{14}{21} \qquad \frac{15}{16} \qquad \frac{21}{25} \qquad \frac{18}{35}$$

Decimals and Percents

For each problem, provide three examples that satisfy the given condition and one that does not.

	Condition	Three	One
1.	**Write four decimals:** three that are decimals for eighths and one that is not.	0.125, 0.375, 0.25	0.16
2.	**Write four decimals:** three that are between 0 and 1 and one that is not.		
3.	**Write four decimals:** three that are terminating decimals and one that is not.		
4.	**Write four percent problems:** three that have an answer of 6 and one that does not.		
5.	**Write four numbers:** three that are equivalent to 350% and one that is not.		
6.	**Write four decimals:** three that are less than 0.5 and one that is not.		
7.	**Write four ratios:** three that are equivalent to 20% and one that is not.		
8.	**Write four simple interest problems:** three that have an interest of $8.00 and one that does not.		

- -

. . . AND THINK

Examine the following set of numbers. Select one of the numbers that does not belong with the other three and state the reason for your selection.

20% of 40   40% of 20   10% of 80   5% of 20

Geometry

For each problem, provide three examples that satisfy the given condition and one that does not. *If you need more space to make drawings, use the back of this page.*

Condition	Three	One
1. **Write four angle measures:** three that are obtuse and one that is not.	91°, 179°, 125°	20°
2. **Write four pairs of angle measures:** three that are complementary and one that is not.		
3. **Write four names of polygons:** three that are quadrilaterals and one that is not.		
4. **Write four sets of three angle measures:** three that represent the angles of a triangle and one that does not.		
5. **Write four types of triangles:** three that represent the classification of triangles by sides and one that does not.		
6. **Draw four figures:** three that have a perimeter of 12 units and one that does not.		
7. **Draw four figures:** three that have an area of 20 square units and one that does not.		
8. **Write four sets of three numbers:** three that are Pythagorean triples and one that is not.		

. . . AND THINK

Examine the following set of terms. Select one of the terms that does not belong with the other three and state the reason for your selection.

acute   scalene   right   obtuse

MATH INTERSECTIONS © Dale Seymour Publications

Measurement

For each problem, provide three examples that satisfy the given condition and one that does not.

	Condition	Three	One
1.	**Write four units of measure:** three that are linear and one that is not.	feet, yard, inch	quart
2.	**Write four units of measure:** three that are metric and one that is not.		
3.	**Write four units of measure:** three that are measures of capacity and one that is not.		
4.	**Write four measures:** three that are equivalent to 2 yards and one that is not.		
5.	**Write four measures:** three that are equivalent to 1 meter and one that is not.		
6.	**Write four measures:** three that are equivalent to 1 square meter and one that is not.		
7.	**Write four measures:** three that are markings on a ruler and one that is not.		
8.	**List four devices:** three that are used to measure and one that is not.		

- -

. . . AND THINK

Examine the following set of values. Select one of the values that does not belong with the other three and state the reason for your selection.

$$100 \qquad 6 \text{ dozen} \qquad \frac{1}{2} \text{ gross} \qquad 72$$

Pre-Algebra

For each problem, provide three examples that satisfy the given condition and one that does not.

	Condition	Three	One
1.	**Write four ordered pairs:** three that are in the first quadrant and one that is not.	(2,2) (3,5) (1,4)	(-1, 2)
2.	**Write four numbers:** three that have a reciprocal and one that does not.		
3.	**Write four numbers:** three that are greater than ⁻4 and one that is not.		
4.	**Write four pairs of numbers:** three that are opposites and one that is not.		
5.	**Write four exponential expressions:** three that are square expressions and one that is not.		
6.	**Write four exponential expressions:** three that have a value of 64 and one that does not.		
7.	**Write four numbers:** three that are solutions to $x + 4 < 3$ and one that is not.		
8.	**Write four terms for variables:** three that are similar terms and one that is not.		

■ ■

. . . AND THINK

Examine the following set of numbers. Select one of the numbers that does not belong with the other three and state the reason for your selection.

$$\sqrt{18} \qquad \sqrt{32} \qquad \sqrt{48} \qquad \sqrt{50}$$

MATH INTERSECTIONS © Dale Seymour Publications

Section 2
Sometimes

Introduction

The *Sometimes* activity is designed to focus students on a condition that is true in some cases but not in others. It is important for students to understand that for a statement to be true, it must be true under all conditions. This activity provides a more effective format than true/false or sometimes/always/never questions because it is not possible for students to guess. In this activity, the student will be expected to provide examples that illustrate when the given condition is true and when it is false.

SAMPLE EXERCISES

Each condition given below is true in some cases and false in at least one instance. For each situation presented, provide an example of when the condition is true and one that shows when the condition is false. Your answer may be a diagram, numerical expression, or written response.

	Condition	True	False
1.	50% is equal to 50.	base is 100	base is 50
2.	The sum of the measures of two acute angles is an obtuse angle.	Angle = 60° Angle = 70°	Angle = 30° Angle = 40°

To conclude each page, the students are asked in the *STOP . . . AND THINK* activity to generate any statement, within the category, that is true all of the time. These statements are likely to be definitions, properties, or theorems. For example, in the "Geometry" category, the student might offer the statement "the acute angles of a right triangle are complementary." In the "Pre-Algebra" category, the student might offer the statement "$a(b + c) = ab + ac$."

Number Theory

Each condition given below is true in some cases and false in at least one instance. For each situation presented, provide an example of when the condition is true and one that shows when the condition is false. Your answer may be a diagram, numerical expression, or written response.

Condition	True	False
1. Prime numbers are odd.	3	2
2. The greatest common factor of two numbers is less than either number.		
3. When you double a number, the result is even.		
4. When you raise 3 to a power, the ones digit in the result is a 3 or a 9.		
5. The least common multiple of two odd numbers is the product of the two numbers.		
6. Numbers have an even number of factors.		
7. A whole number is either prime or composite.		
8. The cube of a number is greater than the square of a number.		

- -

. . . AND THINK

Using the topic of this page, write a statement that is always true. Be prepared to justify your response.

Fractions, Decimals, and Percents

Each condition given below is true in some cases and false in at least one instance. For each situation presented, provide an example of when the condition is true and one that shows when the condition is false. Your answer may be a diagram, numerical expression, or written response.

	Condition	True	False
1.	The reciprocal of a number is a fraction.	reciprocal of 3 is $\frac{1}{3}$	reciprocal of $\frac{1}{4}$ is 4
2.	A number has a reciprocal.		
3.	A fraction with a denominator of 6 has a smaller value than a fraction with a denominator of 4.		
4.	A decimal with a 5 in the tenths place is less than a decimal with a 3 in the hundredths place.		
5.	The product of two decimals is a decimal.		
6.	The sum of two fractions is a fraction.		
7.	20% of a number is greater than 10% of a different number.		
8.	The percent of a number must be less than or equal to the number.		

. . . AND THINK
Using the topic of this page, write a statement that is always true. Be prepared to justify your response.

MATH INTERSECTIONS © Dale Seymour Publications

Geometry

Each condition given below is true in some cases and false in at least one instance. For each situation presented, provide an example of when the condition is true and one that shows when the condition is false. Your answer may be a diagram, numerical expression, or written response.

	Condition	True	False
1.	A rectangle is a square.		
2.	A rhombus is a square.		
3.	An equiangular polygon is regular.		
4.	An isosceles triangle is acute.		
5.	If two circles have the same center, they must be the same circle.		
6.	If *B* is between *A* and *C*, and *E* is between *C* and *D*, then *E* is between *A* and *B*.		

. . . AND THINK
Using the topic of this page, write a statement that is always true. Be prepared to justify your response.

Geometry

Each condition given below is true in some cases and false in at least one instance. For each situation presented, provide an example of when the condition is true and one that shows when the condition is false. Your answer may be a diagram, numerical expression, or written response.

	Condition	True	False
1.	Two supplementary angles are congruent.	$m<1 = 90°$ $m<2 = 90°$	$m<1 = 30°$ $m<2 = 150°$
2.	The supplement of an angle is acute.		
3.	The altitudes of a triangle are inside the triangle.		
4.	Similar triangles are congruent.		
5.	The two nonparallel sides of a trapezoid are congruent.		
6.	The diagonals of a quadrilateral bisect each other.		
7.	If a line bisects a line segment, it is perpendicular to the line segment.		
8.	A line intersects a circle in two points.		

. . . AND THINK

Using the topic of this page, write a statement that is always true. Be prepared to justify your response.

Pre-Algebra

Each condition given below is true in some cases and false in at least one instance. For each situation presented, provide an example of when the condition is true and one that shows when the condition is false. Your answer may be a diagram, numerical expression, or written response.

Condition	True	False
1. $\|a + b\| = \|a\| + \|b\|$	$\|2+3\| = \|2\|+\|3\|$	$\|2+^-3\| \neq \|2\|+\|^-3\|$
2. $(a + b)^2 = a^2 + b^2$		
3. Numbers are either positive or negative.		
4. The product of an even number of factors is positive.		
5. $^-1$ to a power yields a negative answer.		
6. $x^2 = 2x$		
7. If the x and y coordinates of a point have the same sign, the point is in the first quadrant.		
8. $\sqrt{a + b} = \sqrt{a} + \sqrt{b}$		

- -

. . . AND THINK

Using the topic of this page, write a statement that is always true. Be prepared to justify your response.

Miscellaneous

Each condition given below is true in some cases and false in at least one instance. For each situation presented, provide an example of when the condition is true and one that shows when the condition is false. Your answer may be a diagram, numerical expression, or written response.

	Condition	True	False
1.	The average of three numbers is one of the three numbers.	average of 15, 16, and 17 is <u>16</u>	average of 20, 22, and 30 is <u>24</u>
2.	The average of three even numbers is an even number.		
3.	A set of numbers has exactly one mode.		
4.	Any fraction can represent the probability of an event.		
5.	An urn contains red balls, white balls, and blue balls. The probability of selecting a red ball is $\frac{1}{3}$.		
6.	The median of a set of numbers is in the set.		
7.	A probability must be a fraction.		
8.	In a class, ten students are boys and fifteen students have brown hair. There are twenty-five students in the class.		

- -

. . . AND THINK

Using the topic of this page, write a statement that is always true. Be prepared to justify your response.

Section 3
Tell All
You Know

Introduction

The *Tell All You Know* activity allows students to focus on the nature of the problem rather than the answer. The idea is for students to tell you the "things" they know about the problem, but not to provide a specific answer. For example, it may be appropriate for the student to discuss the type of numbers in the problem, the operations used, the relationships, and the expected range for answers. This activity is open-ended and designed to encourage the use of higher-level thinking skills and number sense. In completing the exercises, the student will be able to show his/her ability to communicate mastery of mathematical concepts.

SAMPLE EXERCISES

Study the problems given. List as many things as you can about them. You are *not* expected to find answers to the problems, but rather to list the characteristics you find in them.

Example 1:

Tell all you know about this problem:

1. Find the average of 62, 80, 94.

- The sum will be even.
- The average will be greater than 62.
- The average will be less than 94.
- Three times the average equals the sum of the numbers.

Note: A frequently suggested incorrect statement made my students with regard to this example is that the average is an even number. This need not be the case as the average may not even be a whole number.

Example 2:

Tell all you know about this problem:

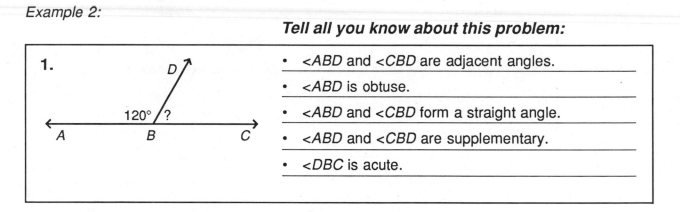

- <*ABD* and <*CBD* are adjacent angles.
- <*ABD* is obtuse.
- <*ABD* and <*CBD* form a straight angle.
- <*ABD* and <*CBD* are supplementary.
- <*DBC* is acute.

To help students attain closure for this activity, the *STOP . . . AND THINK* question asks them to choose the most reasonable answer to a given question from a set of four possible choices. It is expected that students will reflect on key concepts as they answer these multiple-choice questions. For instance, in working with percents, to determine what percent of 30 is 60, students should recognize that the percent sought should be greater than 100% since 60 is greater than 30.

General Note: Encourage students to use the back of the worksheets if they need more space to write. Students may have a lot to tell about some of these problems, and they shouldn't be constrained by the necessarily limited space on the worksheets.

Number Theory

Study the problems given. List as many things as you can about them. You are *not* expected to find answers to the problems, but rather to list the characteristics you find in them.

Tell all you know about this problem:

1. $\sqrt{17} = ?$	$\sqrt{17}$ is less than $\sqrt{25}$. $\sqrt{17}$ is greater than $\sqrt{16}$. $\sqrt{17}$ is not a whole number. $\sqrt{17}$ is between 4 and 5.
2. Find the greatest common factor of 12 and 18.	
3. Find the least common multiple of 4 and 6.	
4. Find the average of 30, 33, and 41.	
5. Find the prime factorization of 36.	
6. What is the value of 2.5×10^3?	

. . . AND THINK

Without doing the problem, which answer choice is the most reasonable? Explain the reasons for the choice you made.

The average of 19, 26, 27, and 28 is

        a. 12   b. 20.3   c. 25   d. 100

Fractions and Decimals

Study the problems given. List as many things as you can about them. You are *not* expected to find answers to the problems, but rather to list the characteristics you find in them.

Tell all you know about this problem:

1. $\frac{1}{2} + \frac{2}{3}$	The sum is greater than 1. The common denominator is 6. The sum is greater than $\frac{1}{2} + \frac{1}{2}$. The sum is not $\frac{3}{5}$.
2. $4\frac{1}{2} \times 5$	
3. $4 \div \frac{1}{2}$	
4. 16×3.12	
5. $0.3 + 0.7 + 0.5$	
6. 4.8×100	

. . . AND THINK

Without doing the problem, which answer choice is the most reasonable? Explain the reasons for the choice you made.

$0.3 + 0.5 + 0.7 =$

     a. 0.15   b. 1.5   c. 15   d. 0.015

Percents

Study the problems given. List as many things as you can about them. You are *not* expected to find answers to the problems, but rather to list the characteristics you find in them.

Tell all you know about this problem:

1.	What is 150% of 60?	The answer is greater than 60. The answer is the same as 60 + 30. The answer is less than 120. The answer is equivalent to 100% of 60 plus 50% of 60.
2.	87% of 10 is what number?	
3.	What percent of 15 is 45?	
4.	$\frac{1}{2}$ % of 200 is what number?	
5.	Which is larger, 6% of 120 or 12% of 50?	
6.	27% of what number is 8?	

- -

. . . AND THINK

Without doing the problem, which answer choice is the most reasonable? Explain the reasons for the choice you made.

What percent of 30 is 60?

      a. 50%   b. 5%   c. 200%   d. 18%

Geometry

Study the diagrams given. List as many things as you can about them. You are *not* expected to find answers to the problems, but rather to list the characteristics you find in them.

Tell all you know about this problem:

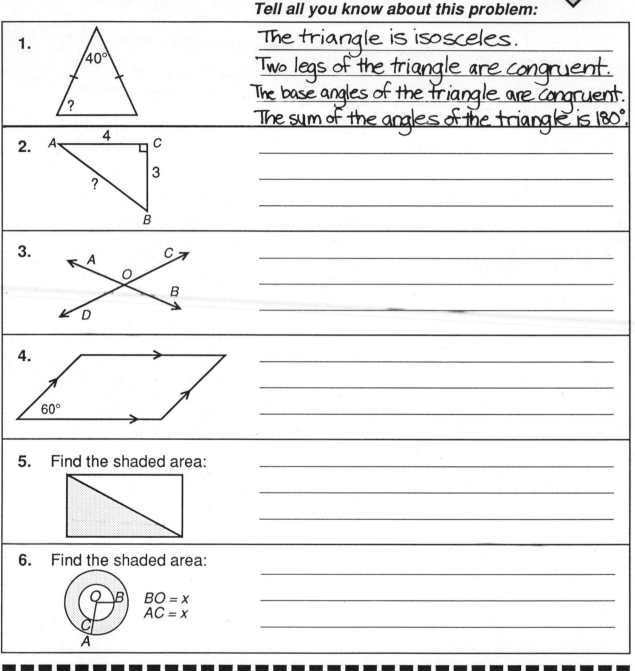

1.

The triangle is isosceles.
Two legs of the triangle are congruent.
The base angles of the triangle are congruent.
The sum of the angles of the triangle is 180°.

2.

3.

4.

5. Find the shaded area:

6. Find the shaded area:

$BO = x$
$AC = x$

STOP

. . . AND THINK

Without doing the problem, which answer choice is the most reasonable? Explain the reasons for the choice you made.

What does the middle angle measure?

a. 82°   b. 41°   c. 8°   d. 18°

MATH INTERSECTIONS © Dale Seymour Publications

Geometry

Study the problems given. List as many things as you can about them. You are *not* expected to find answers to the problems, but rather to list the characteristics you find in them.

Tell all you know about this problem:

---

1. Find the area of the shaded sector of the circle.

   o ⌐ *r* =10

   The central angle is 90° or ¼ of the circle.
   The formula for the area of the circle is A =πr².
   The radius is 10.
   The diameter is 20.

---

2. The squares are congruent. The area of the entire figure is 80.
   Find the perimeter.

   _____
   _____
   _____

---

3. 4 3 5 similar to ? 10

   _____
   _____
   _____

---

4. 40° *l₁*   ? *l₂*

   _____
   _____
   _____

---

5. Find *x*:

   80°   40°   *x°*

   _____
   _____
   _____

---

6. Find the area of the total figure.

   10   10   10   10

   _____
   _____
   _____

. . . AND THINK

Without doing the problem, which answer choice is the most reasonable? Explain the reasons for the choice you made.

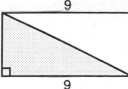

What is the area of the shaded region?

a. 36   b. 18   c. 26   d. 13

MATH INTERSECTIONS © Dale Seymour Publications

Pre-Algebra

Study the problems given. List as many things as you can about them. You are *not* expected to find answers to the problems, but rather to list the characteristics you find in them.

Tell all you know about this problem:

1.	Solve for *x*: $5x + 6 = 20$.	x is positive. $5x = 14$. x is not a whole number.
2.	Simplify: $5x^2 + 4x + 3y^2 + 2y + 6x^2 - 4x$.	
3.	Simplify: $3x(2x + 4y + 6)$.	
4.	Solve for *x*: $5x + 26 = 20$.	
5.	Find the value of $3x^4$ when $x = ^-2$.	
6.	Where does the line $3x - 4y = 12$ cross the *x*-axis?	

STOP

. . . AND THINK

Without doing the problem, which answer choice is the most reasonable? Explain the reasons for the choice you made.

What is the value of $(^-2)^8$?

a. 256   b. 16   c. $^-256$ d. $^-16$

Section 4
What and Why

Introduction

The *What and Why* activity has students focus on the process used in solving a problem. The ability to communicate the process and to provide a rationale for why that process was followed better demonstrates how well the student comprehends the application of key mathematical concepts than does a mechanical completion of the problem. In these exercises, students will tell what they would do to solve the problems and state reasons for why they would proceed that way. Students need to be aware that a given problem may be approached in different ways. The resulting What and Why statements from different solutions can be compared and contrasted. Students may find it difficult to express the Why portion of the activity. Working through several examples as a class may be beneficial.

SAMPLE EXERCISES

For each exercise, state *what* you would do to solve the problem. Be as specific as possible. Then state *why* you would use that process to find the answer.

Exercise	What	Why
1. $\frac{2}{3} + \frac{3}{4}$	I would find the least common denominator for 3 and 4, rewrite the fractions having that denominator, and then add the numerators to complete the problem.	To add fractions with unlike denominators, you must rewrite them with like denominators.
2. $3(4 + 5)$	Add 4 and 5; multiply the sum by 3. – or – Multiply 3 and 4 and 3 and 5, and find the sum.	In order of operations, expressions in parentheses are simplified before the product is found. The distributive property allows you to multiply each term in parentheses by the outside factor before adding.

Alternate solutions should be presented and discussed where appropriate.

To summarize this activity, the *STOP . . . AND THINK* problem asks students to identify a concept they used to answer one of the questions on the page. For example, in "Fractions," the students may respond with the concept of "changing a mixed number to an improper fraction" for question 4 or the concept of "dividing by the greatest common factor" for question 3. There is no one correct response for any of these summary questions. Any appropriate concept the students use should be considered valid.

General Note: Encourage students to use the back of the worksheets if they need more space to write.

Number Theory

For each exercise, state *what* you would do to solve the problem. Be as specific as possible. Then state *why* you would use that process to find the answer.

Exercise	What	Why
1. Find the greatest common factor of 12 and 30.	List the factors of each number; find the common factors; select the largest.	GCF is the largest number that evenly divides two or more numbers.
2. Find the least common multiple of 8 and 12.		
3. Find the prime factorization of 36.		
4. List all the factors of 24.		
5. Estimate $\sqrt{21}$.		
6. Using divisibility tests, is 234 divisible by 6?		

▪ ▪

. . . AND THINK

Identify one mathematical concept used to solve a problem on this page.

Fractions

For each exercise, state *what* you would do to solve the problem. Be as specific as possible. Then state *why* you would use that process to find the answer.

Exercise	What	Why
1. $5\frac{1}{8} - 3\frac{7}{8}$	Regroup 1 from 5 and express it as $\frac{8}{8}$ to give $4\frac{9}{8}$; subtract.	You don't have enough 8ths to subtract. $1 = \frac{8}{8}$.
2. $\frac{7}{8} \div \frac{15}{16}$		
3. Reduce $\frac{18}{24}$		
4. $2\frac{1}{2} \times 3\frac{1}{5}$		
5. $\frac{3}{5}$ of 30		
6. $\frac{5}{8} = \frac{x}{24}$ $x =$		

- -

STOP

. . . AND THINK

Identify one mathematical concept used to solve a problem on this page.

Decimals

For each exercise, state *what* you would do to solve the problem. Be as specific as possible. Then state *why* you would use that process to find the answer.

Exercise	What	Why
1. $12 + 3.95 + 0.75$	Line up the decimal points; add.	Place value requires the decimals to be aligned.
2. $17 - 14.98$		
3. 6.2×1000		
4. $4.8 \div 0.4$		
5. Change $\frac{3}{5}$ to a decimal.		
6. $452 \div 100$		

- -

. . . AND THINK

Identify one mathematical concept used to solve a problem on this page.

Percents

For each exercise, state *what* you would do to solve the problem. Be as specific as possible. Then state *why* you would use that process to find the answer.

Exercise	What	Why
1. Find $33\frac{1}{3}\%$ of 18.	Change $33\frac{1}{3}\%$ to $\frac{1}{3}$. Then find $\frac{1}{3}$ of 18.	To find percents of numbers, either the fraction or decimal equivalent is used.
2. Express $\frac{1}{2}\%$ as a decimal.		
3. Change $\frac{7}{8}$ to a percent.		
4. What percent of 25 is 15?		
5. 20% of a number is 7. What is the number?		
6. A shirt originally priced at $24.00 goes on sale for 25% off. What is the sale price of the shirt?		

■ ■

. . . AND THINK

Identify one mathematical concept used to solve a problem on this page.

Geometry

For each exercise, state *what* you would do to solve the problem. Be as specific as possible. Then state *why* you would use that process to find the answer.

Exercise	What	Why
1. Find the perimeter of a regular hexagon with a side measure of 8 inches.	Multiply 6 and 8.	A regular hexagon has 6 congruent sides. The perimeter is the distance around the figure.
2. Find the volume of the figure given.		
3. The outside faces of the cube are painted red. How many faces are unpainted?		
4. Find the area of the given figure.		
5. Find the area of the shaded region.		
6. Find the perimeter of the given figure.		

. . . AND THINK

Identify one mathematical concept used to solve a problem on this page.

Pre-Algebra

For each exercise, state *what* you would do to solve the problem. Be as specific as possible. Then state *why* you would use that process to find the answer.

Exercise	What	Why
1. Find the value of x^2 when $x = {}^-5$.	Substitute $^-5$ for X. Then multiply $^-5 \times {}^-5$.	To evaluate an expression, you substitute a given value for the variable and apply order of operations.
2. Solve $2x + 7 = 15$.		
3. $16 - ({}^-4)$		
4. $(5)(8) - (6)(3)$		
5. Graph $2x + y = 7$.		
6. Simplify $\sqrt{200}$.		

■ ■

STOP

. . . AND THINK

Identify one mathematical concept used to solve a problem on this page.

Section 5
One Picture
Is Worth
1,000 Words

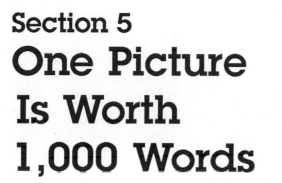

Introduction

The *One Picture Is Worth 1,000 Words* activity has students
demonstrate their understanding of problem settings and suggested
relationships by drawing a diagram to depict a given situation. The
difficulty students often have in solving problems results from their
inability to draw an appropriate diagram that represents the problem.
The clarity and completeness of the diagram should communicate how
well the student comprehends the problem. It is not expected that
students will find the answer to the problem. The focus should be on
the diagram only. In some problems, it is necessary to label the diagram
to reflect given information.

SAMPLE EXERCISES

Draw a diagram or picture to represent the situation described in each problem. You should label your diagram with data contained in the problem. *Do not attempt to find an answer to the problem.* Your attention should be given to the concepts and relationships described in the statement of the problem.

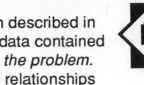

Example 1:

If five distinct rays have a common endpoint, how many pairs of adjacent angles exist?

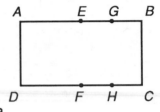

Example 2:

ABCD is a rectangle with area equal to 48 square inches. *E* is the midpoint of *AB*, *F* is the midpoint of *CD*, *G* is the midpoint of *EB*, and *H* is the midpoint of *CF*. What is the area of rectangle *GBCH*?

> To provide closure for this activity, the *STOP . . . AND THINK* exercise on each page asks the student to select any problem from the page, and, with a partner, describe two pieces of critical information. Critical information can be a relationship that exists within the diagram. For example, in the *STOP . . . AND THINK* exercise for "Geometry—Angles, Segments, Lines," problem number 3 could have students indicate (a) the endpoints are located ten units to the left and ten units to the right (4,2); (b) the *y* coordinates will be the same, since the segment is horizontal.

> ***General Note:*** *Encourage students to use the back of the worksheets if they need more space to draw. Students may want to make large diagrams to represent the situations described in certain problems, and they shouldn't be constrained by the necessarily limited space on the worksheets.*

Fractions and Percents

Draw a diagram or picture to represent the situation described in each problem. You should label your diagram with data contained in the problem. *Do not attempt to find an answer to the problem.* Your attention should be given to the concepts and relationships described in the statement of the problem.

1. Show that 4 divided by $\frac{1}{2}$ is 8.

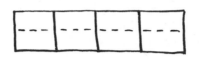

2. Show that $\frac{1}{2}$ % does not equal 50%.

3. Show that 50% is not always 50.

4. Show that 25% of 50 has the same result as 50% of 25.

5. Show that $4\frac{1}{2}$ x 6 is not $24\frac{1}{2}$.

6. Show that 30% of some amount is the same as three times 10% of the same amount.

. . . AND THINK

Select a problem from the page. Working with a partner, indicate two critical pieces of information represented in the diagram.

Geometry—Angles, Segments, Lines

Draw a diagram or picture to represent the situation described in each problem. You should label your diagram with data contained in the problem. *Do not attempt to find an answer to the problem.* Your attention should be given to the concepts and relationships described in the statement of the problem.

1. In a plane, line *a* is perpendicular to line *b*.
    Line *b* is perpendicular to line *c*.
    Line *d* is perpendicular to line *c*.
    What is the relationship of line *a* to line *c*?

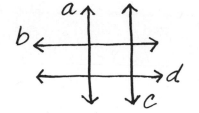

2. In a plane, three lines intersect at a point. How many different pairs of vertical angles are formed?

3. A horizontal line segment has a midpoint of (4,2). If the length of the segment is 20 units, what are the coordinates of the endpoints of the segment?

4. Two adjacent angles form a straight angle. Each of these two angles is bisected. What is the measure of the angle formed by these bisectors?

5. *A* is the midpoint of segment *BC, D* is the midpoint of segment *AB, E* is the midpoint of segment *BD,* and *F* is the midpoint of segment *BE.* If *BF* has a length of 3 centimeters, what is the length of *CA*?

6. Three parallel lines are cut by a transversal. How many different pairs of alternate interior angles are formed?

■ ■

. . . AND THINK

Select a problem from the page. Working with a partner, indicate two critical pieces of information represented in the diagram.

 MATH INTERSECTIONS © Dale Seymour Publications

Geometry—Triangles

Draw a diagram or picture to represent the situation described in each problem. You should label your diagram with data contained in the problem. *Do not attempt to find an answer to the problem.* Your attention should be given to the concepts and relationships described in the statement of the problem.

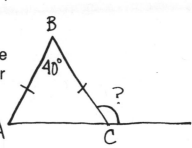

1. Triangle *ABC* is an isosceles triangle. The measure of the vertex angle *B* is 40°. What is the measure of the exterior angle at *C*?

2. Can an altitude of a triangle fall outside the triangle?

3. The vertices of an isosceles triangle are (2,0), (10,0), and (6,6). What is the area of the triangle?

4. A 25-foot ladder is placed against a wall. It forms an angle of 30° with the wall. How far up the wall does the ladder reach?

5. Each side of an equilateral triangle is 8 inches long. A small equilateral triangle with side length of 1 inch is cut from each corner of the original triangle. What is the perimeter of the resulting figure?

6. Two isosceles triangles share a common base but do not share any area. The sides of one triangle measure 5 inches, 5 inches, and 3 inches; the sides of the second triangle measure 10 inches, 10 inches, and 3 inches. What is the perimeter of the figure formed by drawing the two triangles?

■■■ ■■■ ■■■ ■■■ ■■■ ■■■ ■■■ ■■■ ■■■ ■■■ ■■■ ■■ ■

. . . AND THINK
Select a problem from the page. Working with a partner, indicate two critical pieces of information represented in the diagram.

Geometry—Rectangles and Squares

Draw a diagram or picture to represent the situation described in each problem. You should label your diagram with data contained in the problem. *Do not attempt to find an answer to the problem.* Your attention should be given to the concepts and relationships described in the statement of the problem.

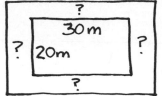

1. A rectangular garden is 20 meters by 30 meters. The garden is surrounded by a path of uniform width. If the total area of the garden and the path is 936 square meters, how wide is the path?

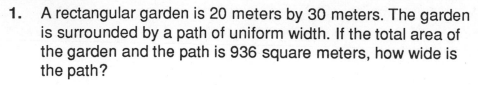

2. A 1 x 1 small square is cut from each corner of an 8 x 8 checkerboard. What is the perimeter of the resulting figure?

3. Each side of one square is twice as long as each side of a smaller square. If the area of the smaller square is 25 square feet, what is the perimeter of the larger square?

4. A rectangular piece of paper, folded in half, forms a square with a perimeter of 32 centimeters. Find the area of the original rectangle.

5. A rectangle has four vertices. Three of them are (5,1), (5,7), and (10,7). Find the coordinates of the fourth vertex.

6. A square has one vertex at (0,0). Find the coordinates of the other three vertices if the area of the square is 25 square units.

. . . AND THINK

Select a problem from the page. Working with a partner, indicate two critical pieces of information represented in the diagram.

Miscellaneous

Draw a diagram or picture to represent the situation described in each problem. You should label your diagram with data contained in the problem. *Do not attempt to find an answer to the problem.* Your attention should be given to the concepts and relationships described in the statement of the problem.

1. The temperature started at 2° C and dropped three degrees in each of the next four hours. How much below 0° C was the final temperature at the end of a four-hour period?

2. According to a scale on a road map, 2 centimeters represents 10 kilometers. If two cities are 24 centimeters apart on the map, what is the actual distance between them?

3. Two concentric circles are such that the radius of one is twice the radius of the other.

4. How many different ways can five postage stamps be attached to one another?

5. Eight people are in a single elimination tournament. Show the possible pairings.

6. How many different towers can be built with three different-colored cubes: a red cube, a blue cube, and a white cube? (Each tower should include all three cubes.)

■■■ ■■■■ ■■ ■■ ■■■■ ■ ■ ■ ■■ ■ ■■ ■■ ■■ ■■■ ■■ ■■ ■■ ■ ■

. . . AND THINK

Select a problem from the page. Working with a partner, indicate two critical pieces of information represented in the diagram.

Miscellaneous

Draw a diagram or picture to represent the situation described in each problem. You should label your diagram with data contained in the problem. *Do not attempt to find an answer to the problem.* Your attention should be given to the concepts and relationships described In the statement of the problem.

1. Fencing is placed around a rectangular plot that measures 15 feet by 20 feet. If the posts are placed every 5 feet, how many posts are used?

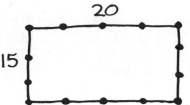

2. On a number line, point A has coordinate $5\frac{1}{2}$ and point B has coordinate $-2\frac{1}{2}$. What is the coordinate on the number line that is equidistant from A and B?

3. Show that the square of a sum is not equal to the sum of the individual squares.

4. There are three roads from town P to town Q and five other roads from town Q to town R. Mr. Jones must drive from town P to town R by way of town Q. How many different routes are possible?

5. Two cars start at the same point and travel in opposite directions. One travels an average of 55 mph and the other 48 mph. How long will it take for them to be 397 miles apart?

6. A square is drawn around a circle such that the circle touches the sides of the square. What percent of the area of the square is outside the circle?

■ ■

. . . AND THINK

Select a problem from the page. Working with a partner, indicate two critical pieces of information represented in the diagram.

Section 6
Dictionary Revisited

Introduction

The *Dictionary Revisited* activities are a potpourri of exercises that focus on the terminology of mathematics. These exercises focus on the meanings of terms and concepts, the application of concepts, the relationship among concepts, the recognition of concepts, and the general command of a mathematical vocabulary. The section contains six different exercise sets: "Analogies," "Adjectives," "How Many?", "What Comes Next?", "Opposites," and "Insert a Word."

SAMPLE EXERCISES

Analogies: In this activity, students are expected to complete the given analogy. They must be able to determine the relationship among the terms and concepts given. Following the completion of the analogies, it is important to discuss with students what the relationships are and how they are determined.

Example: $2\pi r$: circumference : : πr^2 : ???
Answer: area

Adjectives: In this activity, students are expected to provide a mathematical phrase in which the given adjective is used. More than one answer may be possible. If phrases can be found in different areas of mathematics, encourage students to provide multiple answers.

Example: prime
Answer: prime number, prime factor

How Many?: In this activity, students are asked to provide a numerical answer. To determine the answer, students must know the terminology used and the concepts referred to.

Example: How many *diagonals* does a *pentagon* have?
Answer: **5**

What Comes Next?: In this activity, students are asked to complete a given sequence with the term or number that comes next. The relationship of the terms given must be determined to complete the problem.

Example: ones, tens, hundreds, thousands, ???
Answer: ten thousands

Opposites: In this activity, students are asked to provide the opposite of the concept presented—and an example of both the concept and the opposite. Discuss with students the meanings of the original term and the opposite provided. Note that the word associations generated in this activity are not always opposites in the true sense. Rather, they may be *contrasting* pairs of concepts.

Example: odd—3
Answer: even—2

Insert a Word: In this activity, students are asked to insert a word or phrase that results in making the given statement true all of the time.

Example: Corresponding sides of two triangles are proportional.
Answer: Corresponding sides of two *similar* triangles are proportional.

To provide closure for this section, the *STOP . . . AND THINK* activity at the bottom of each page asks students to create an original example similar to the ones presented on the page. For instance, on the page, "Analogies," students are asked to generate an original analogy from any area of mathematics. These original examples should be shared through small group and/or total class discussion.

42

Analogies

Complete each analogy so the relationship that exists between the second pair is the same as the relationship that exists between the first pair.

1. multiplication : addition :: division: <u>subtraction</u>

2. meter : yard :: liter: _____

3. four : cardinal :: fourth: _____

4. polygon : perimeter :: circle: _____

5. one-half : terminating decimal :: one-third: _____

6. 90° : complementary :: 180°: _____

7. area : square units :: volume: _____

8. circle : sphere :: square: _____

9. V : 5 :: X: _____

10. $12\frac{1}{2}$ % : $\frac{1}{8}$ :: $37\frac{1}{2}$ %: _____

11. 37° : acute :: 112°: _____

12. 654 : 6.54 x 10² :: 0.273: _____

- -

. . . AND THINK

Write an original analogy using the same form as used on this page. Your analogy can come from any area of mathematics.

Adjectives

Each of the following is an adjective used in connection with a familiar mathematical term. Complete the phrase by adding the missing term. Think of as many phrases as you can using the adjective provided—and illustrate at least one of the phrases with a diagram or written explanation.

Adjectives	Complete Phrases	Illustrations
1. isosceles	isosceles triangle isosceles trapezoid	a △ a b
2. linear		
3. right		
4. similar		
5. parallel		
6. vertical		
7. obtuse		
8. corresponding		
9. regular		
10. square		
11. rectangular		
12. concentric		

- -

. . . AND THINK

List two other adjectives used in mathematical terms. Give the adjective and the phrases.

How Many?

Answer the following questions.

How Many . . .

1.	degrees in a circle?	360°
2.	lines of symmetry in a square?	
3.	diagonals in a square?	
4.	diameters in a circle?	
5.	vertices in a cube?	
6.	fractions between $\frac{1}{2}$ and $\frac{1}{3}$?	
7.	whole-number factors of 36?	
8.	two-digit multiples of 13?	
9.	palindromes between 100 and 200?	
10.	square feet in a square yard?	
11.	numbers have an absolute value equal to 5?	
12.	quarter-ounces in a pound?	

- -

. . . AND THINK

List another problem similar to the ones presented on this page. Provide the related question and the numerical answer to the "How Many?" question.

What Comes Next?

Each of the following represents a sequential pattern. Supply the next number or word to continue the pattern.

1. penny, nickel, dime, ___quarter___

2. triangle, quadrilateral, pentagon, hexagon, _____

3. thirds, fourths, fifths, sixths, _____

4. meter, decameter, hectometer, _____

5. tenth, hundredth, thousandth, _____

6. X, XX, XXX, XL, _____

7. 2, 4, 8, 16, _____

8. 10, 100, 1000, _____

9. $\frac{1}{3}, \frac{1}{9}, \frac{1}{27},$ _____

10. 2, 3, 5, 7, 11, _____

11. 1, 4, 9, 16, _____

12. 1, 8, 27, 64, _____

■-■

. . . AND THINK

Provide another sequential pattern similar to the ones on this page. Your pattern can come from any area of mathematics.

Opposites

For each of the following, write the word that has the opposite or contrasting meaning. Provide an example of each.

Term	Example	Opposite	Example
1. positive	5	negative	$^-5$
2. square (of a number)			
3. prime			
4. vertical			
5. intersecting			
6. interior			
7. double			
8. acute			
9. equation			
10. numerator			
11. rational			
12. terminating			

. . . AND THINK

List two additional opposite (or contrasting) relationships that occur in mathematics. Describe the meaning of the opposites.

Insert a Word

Insert a word or a phrase in order to make each of the following statements always true.

1. Corresponding sides of two triangles are proportional.

   Corresponding sides of two <u>similar</u> triangles are proportional.

2. The cube of a number results in a negative number.

3. Every number has a reciprocal.

4. An altitude of a triangle falls outside the triangle.

5. The sum of odd numbers is even.

6. A triangle is equiangular.

7. Any median of a triangle is also an altitude.

8. A double of a number results in an even number.

9. The reciprocal of a number is greater than the number.

10. The supplement of an angle will be an acute angle.

11. 5% is exactly $5.00.

12. The nonparallel sides of a trapezoid are congruent.

- -

. . . AND THINK
Write an original sentence in which a key word (or words) has been omitted. Have a partner *insert* the necessary word(s) to make your sentence always true.

Answer Section

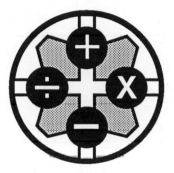

Answer Section

Note: All answers provided here are suggestions. Other answers are possible.

Section 1: Three vs. One

Page 3 (Number Theory)
2. 4, 6, 9; 8 **3.** 12, 24, 36; 16 **4.** 111, 201, 333; 200 **5.** 4, 9, 16; 24 **6.** 1, 8, 27; 100 **7.** 2×10^2, 3.4×10^3, 4.25×10^{-1}; 27×10 **8.** (20, 30), (24, 26), (21,29); (20, 40)

Page 4 (Fractions)
2. 6/16, 9/24, 12/32; 6/24 **3.** 2/3, 3/4, 4/5; 1/3 **4.** 3/2, 4/3, 5/4; 4/5 **5.** 1/8, 1/4, 1/5; 1/3 **6.** 2/3, 3/5, 7/10; 4/5 **7.** (7/8, 1/8), (3/4, 1/4), (2/5, 3/5); (3/8, 7/8) **8.** (3/5, 5/3), (2/3, 3/2), (3/4, 4/3); (3/2, 3/2)

Page 5 (Decimals and Percents)
2. 0.5, 0.75, 0.99; 1.5 **3.** 0.75, 0.4, 0.031; 0.66... **4.** 10% of 60, 60% of 10, 20% of 30; 1% of 60 **5.** 3-1/2, 3.5, 7/2; 0.35 **6.** 0.1, 0.45, 0.003; 0.8 **7.** 1/5, 20/100, 2/10; 2/5 **8.** $100.00 at 8% for 1 year, $100.00 at 4% for 2 years, $50.00 at 8% for 2 years; $100.00 at 6% for 1 year

Page 6 (Geometry)
2. (20°, 70°), (40°, 50°), (45°, 45°); (40°, 60°) **3.** rectangle, square, rhombus; pentagon **4.** (50°, 60°, 70°), (100°, 30°, 50°), (30°, 60°, 90°); (60°, 70°, 80°) **5.** scalene, isosceles, equilateral; acute **6.** rectangle 4 x 2, rectangle 1 x 5, triangle 4 x 4 x 4; triangle 2 x 2 x 2 **7.** rectangle 4 x 5, triangle: base of 8, height of 5, rectangle 2 x 10; square 4 x 4 **8.** (3, 4, 5), (5, 12, 13), (6, 8, 10); (5, 6, 7)

Page 7 (Measurement)
2. meter, gram, liter; foot **3.** quart, gallon, liter; gram **4.** 6 feet, 72 inches, 1 yard and 3 feet; 60 inches **5.** 100 centimeters, 1,000 millimeters, 10 decimeters; 100 millimeters **6.** 10,000 square centimeters, 100 square decimeters, 1,000,000 square millimeters; 100 square centimeters **7.** 1/2 inch, 1/4 inch, 1/8 inch; 1/3 inch **8.** ruler, protractor, balance; compass

Page 8 (Pre-Algebra)
2. 3, ⁻4, 1/2; 0 **3.** ⁻3, 0, 1; ⁻5 **4.** (⁻5,5), (⁻1/2, 1/2) (⁻4.2, 4.2); (3, 1/3) **5.** x^2, $4x^2$, x^2y^2; $3x^3$ **6.** 2^6, 4^3, 8^2; 2^5 **7.** ⁻2, ⁻4, ⁻5; 7 **8.** $3x$, ⁻$5x$, x; x^2

Section 2: Sometimes

Page 11 (Number Theory)
2. *True:* 12, 18; *False:* 4, 8 **3.** *True:* 5; *False:* 1/2 **4.** *True:* 3^2; *False:* 3^3 **5.** *True:* 3, 5; *False:* 3, 9 **6.** *True:* 15; *False:* 16 **7.** *True:* 4; *False:* 1 **8.** *True:* $3^3 > 3^2$; *False:* $(1/2)^3 < (1/2)^2$

Page 12 (Fractions, Decimals, and Percents)
2. *True:* 6; *False:* 0 **3.** *True:* 1/6 < 1/4; *False:* 5/6 > 3/4 **4.** *True:* 0.5 < 0.531; *False:* 0.5 > 0.03 **5.** *True:* (0.3)(0.2); *False:* (0.8)(2.5) **6.** *True:* 1/2 + 1/3 ; *False:* 1/2 + 3/2 **7.** *True:* 20% of 100 > 10% of 50; *False:* 20% of 10 < 10% of 50 **8.** *True:* 50% of 12 < 12; *False:* 150% of 12 > 12

Page 13 (Geometry)

2. *True:* *False:* **3.** *True:* *False:*

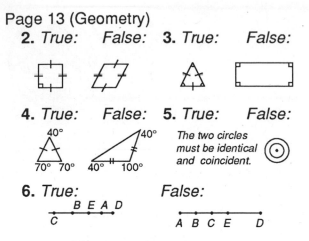

4. *True:* *False:* **5.** *True:* *False:*

40°
70° 70°

40°
40° 100°

The two circles must be identical and coincident.

6. *True:* *False:*

B E A D
C

A B C E   D

Page 14 (Geometry)

2. *True:* The supplement of 150° is 30°; *False:* The supplement of 40° is 140°.

3. *True:* *False:*

4. *True:* *False:*

$3\dfrac{4}{5}$ ~ $3\dfrac{4}{5}$ $3\dfrac{4}{5}$ ~ $6\dfrac{8}{10}$

5. *True:* *False:*

6. *True:* *False:*

7. *True:* *False:* **8.** *True:* *False:*

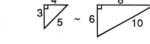

Page 15 (Pre-Algebra)

2. *True:* $(3 + 0)^2 = 3^2 + 0^2$; *False:* $(1 + 1)^2 = 1^2 + 1^2$ **3.** *True:* ⁻4, 4; *False:* 0 **4.** *True:* (⁻2)(⁻3)(⁻4)(⁻5); *False:* (2)(⁻3)(⁻4)(⁻5) **5.** *True:* (⁻1)³; *False:* (⁻1)² **6.** *True:* if $x = 2$; *False:* if $x = 3$ **7.** *True:* (1,1); *False:* (⁻2, ⁻2) **8.** *True:* $\sqrt{9 + 0} = \sqrt{9} + \sqrt{0}$; *False:* $\sqrt{4 + 9} = \sqrt{4} + \sqrt{9}$

Page 16 (Miscellaneous)

2. *True:* 20, 22, 24; *False:* 20, 22, 26 **3.** *True:* 3, 3, 4, 1; *False:* 3, 3, 1, 1 **4.** *True:* 1/2 ; *False:* 3/2 **5.** *True:* if urn contains 1 red, 1 white, and 1 blue ball; *False:* if urn contains 2 red balls, 1 white ball, and 1 blue ball **6.** *True:* 12, 13, 14; *False:* 12, 13, 14, 15 **7.** *True:* probability = 1/2; *False:* probability = 1 **8.** *True:* 10 boys (no brown hair) + 15 girls (all brown hair) = 25 students; *False:* 10 boys (5 brown hair) + 10 girls (all brown hair) = 20 students

Section 3: Tell All You Know

Page 19 (Number Theory)

2. A number divides 12 and 18; the number is less than 12. **3.** The number is greater than or equal to 6; the number is divisible by 4 and 6; the number is even. **4.** The average is between 30 and 41; the average is closer to 30; the average is 1/3 of the sum. **5.** Contains a 2; product of twos and threes. **6.** The expression is in scientific notation; multiply by 1,000; the answer will be larger than 2.5.

Page 20 (Fractions and Decimals)

2. The product is not 20-1/2; the product is greater than 20; the product is less than 25. **3.** Less than 4; represents the number of halves in 4 wholes; answer is not 2. **4.** Greater than 48; less than 64; product has two decimal places. **5.** Greater than 1; answer is in tenths. **6.** The answer will be larger than 400; the answer will be less than 500.

Page 21 (Percents)

2. The answer is less 100%; the answer is greater than 80%; the answer is less than 10; it's the same as 10% of 87.

Page 21 (Percents)—*cont.*
3. Greater than 100%; equivalent to tripling the number. **4.** Less than 1%; not equal to 50%; same as 200% of 1/2. **5.** One percentage is twice the other; 12% of 50 is the same as 50% of 12 and equals 6; 120% of 6 > 6. **6.** The answer is larger than 8; the answer is less than 32.

Page 22 (Geometry)
2. The hypotenuse is greater than 4; the hypotenuse is less than 7; $a^2 + b^2 = c^2$; right triangle. **3.** The vertical angles are equal; pairs of adjacent angles are supplementary; the sum of four angles is 360°. **4.** Opposite sides are parallel and congruent; opposite angles are congruent; sum of the four angles is 360°; the figure is a parallelogram; consecutive angles are supplementary. **5.** The shaded area is half the rectangle; the base of the triangle is the same as the base of the rectangle; the height of the triangle is the same as the width of the rectangle. **6.** The shaded area is equal to the difference of the areas of the two circles; the circles have the same center; the radius of the larger circle is twice the radius of the smaller circle.

Page 23 (Geometry)
2. The perimeter is the distance around the outside; area of one square is 16; the perimeter consists of 12 outside segments. **3.** The sides are proportional; the triangles are right triangles; the hypotenuse of the second is twice the hypotenuse of the first. **4.** Corresponding angles are congruent; alternate interior angles are congruent; adjacent angles are supplementary. **5.** x is an exterior angle of the triangle; measure of the exterior angle is the sum of the remote interior angles; x is

supplementary to the third interior angle; angles of the triangle add to 180°. **6.** The figure consists of a square and two semicircles; the radius of the semicircle is 5; the side of the square is 10.

Page 24 (Pre-Algebra)
2. Consists of x terms, y terms, x^2 terms, and y^2 terms; add coefficients of similar terms; $4x$ and ^-4x are opposite terms. **3.** The $3x$ multiplies the terms in parentheses; the product will have three terms. **4.** x is negative; $5x = ^-6$; the answer is not a whole number. **5.** The exponent of 4 applies to the x and not the 3; the answer will be positive. **6.** The y coordinate will be 0; it does not cross the origin; substitute $y = 0$ to find the x coordinate.

Section 4: What and Why

Page 27 (Number Theory)
2. *What:* List the multiples, find the common multiples, select the least common multiple; *Why:* Least common multiple is the smallest number that both numbers evenly divide. **3.** *What:* Make factor tree for 36 down to successive products until individual factors are primes; *Why:* Prime factorization is expressing the number as a product of powers of primes. **4.** *What:* List numbers beginning with 1 that evenly divide 24. If number divides, list divisor and quotient. Continue until you reach a number already listed; *Why:* Factors are numbers that evenly divide a given number. **5.** *What:* Find two perfect squares that bound 21, list their square roots, determine a reasonable estimate depending on which square 21 is closer to; *Why:* $\sqrt{21}$ represents the number that, when multiplied by itself, is 21. **6.** *What:* Check if the sum of the digits is divisible

Page 27 (Number Theory)—*cont.*
by 3 and the number is even; *Why:* To
be divisible by 6, the number must be
divisible by 3 and 2.

Page 28 (Fractions)
2. *What:* Rewrite as multiplication using
the reciprocal of the divisor; *Why:*
When dividing two fractions, the divisor
is inverted and the product of the dividend and the reciprocal is found.
3. *What:* Divide numerator and denominator by 6; *Why:* To reduce, divide the
numerator and denominator by the
greatest common factor. **4.** *What:*
Rewrite mixed numbers as improper
fractions and multiply; *Why:* Changing to
improper fractions eliminates the need
to use the distributive property.
5. *What:* Find 1/5 of 30 and multiply by
3; *Why:* 3/5 is 3 x 1/5. **6.** *What:* To find
x, multiply 5 by 3; *Why:* In this proportion, the second denominator is three
times the first—so the second numerator is three times the first numerator.

Page 29 (Decimals)
2. *What:* Line up decimal points, display
two zeros as placeholders to the right
of the decimal point for 17, regroup, and
subtract; *Why:* Place value requires that
decimals be aligned. **3.** *What:* Move
the decimal point three places to the
right; *Why:* Place value requires one
movement of the decimal to the right for
every factor of 10. **4.** *What:* Move
decimal one place to the right in both
the divisor and dividend; divide; *Why:*
To divide decimals, the divisor must be
converted to a whole number; moving
the decimal in the dividend must be
done to compensate for the movement
in the divisor. **5.** *What:* Divide the
denominator into the numerator; *Why:* A
fraction is an indicated quotient.
6. *What:* Move decimal point two places

to the left; *Why:* Place value requires
one move left for every factor of 10 in
the divisor.

Page 30 (Percents)
2. *What:* 1% as a decimal is 0.01, so
1/2% as a decimal is 1/2 of 0.01 or
0.005; *Why:* Halves of equal quantities
are equal. **3.** *What:* Set up the proportion 7/8 = *x*/100) and solve for *x*; *Why:*
The question is asking for the equivalent
ratio to 7/8 with a denominator of 100.
4. *What:* Set up the proportion *x*/100 =
15/25) and solve for *x*; *Why:* The question is asking for the equivalent ratio to
15/25 with a denominator of 100.
5. *What:* Set up the proportion 20/100 =
7/*x* and solve for *x*; *Why:* The question
is asking for the equivalent ratio to
20/100 with a numerator of 7. **6.** *What:*
Find 75% of $24.00; *Why:* The sale
price represents 100% of the original
price − 25% of the original price, or 75%
of the original price.

Page 31 (Geometry)
2. *What:* Use 1/3 of $\pi r^2 h$ to find the
volume of the cone and $\pi r^2 h$ to find the
volume of the cylinder; add the two
answers; *Why:* Volume of the whole is
equal to the sum of the volumes of the
parts. **3.** *What:* Determine the number
of interior faces; *Why:* The paint is
placed only on exterior faces. **4.** *What:*
Subdivide the figure into rectangular
regions; find these areas; add; *Why:*
The area of the whole is equal to the
sum of the areas of the parts. **5.** *What:*
Find the areas of the exterior rectangle
and the interior rectangle; subtract the
two areas; *Why:* The shaded area
represents the difference of the two
areas. **6.** *What:* Find the sum of all
exterior segments; *Why:* Perimeter is
the total distance around the figure.

Page 32 (Pre-Algebra)

2. *What:* Add ⁻7 to both sides and divide both sides by 2; *Why:* In order to isolate the variable, you do the inverse operation in the inverse order from that represented in the equation. **3.** *What:* Add the opposite of ⁻4 to 16; *Why:* By definition, subtraction is addition of the opposite. **4.** *What:* Find the products of 5 and 8 and 3 and 6; find the difference; *Why:* Order of operations. **5.** *What:* Find two ordered pairs of points that satisfy the equation; plot them; draw the line that passes through the points; *Why:* A linear equation requires two points to determine a line. If the coordinates satisfy the equation, they are on the line. **6.** *What:* Express 200 as a product using the largest perfect square that is a factor of 200; find the square root of the perfect square; rewrite with that square root, multiplying the other factor in radical notation; *Why:* $\sqrt{ab} = \sqrt{a} \times \sqrt{b}$.

Section 5: One Picture Is Worth 1,000 Words

Page 35 (Fractions and Percents)

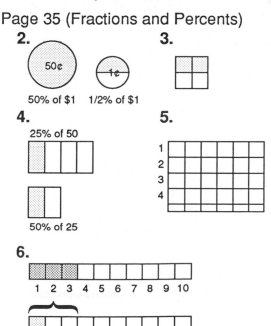

Page 36 (Geometry—Angles, Segments, Lines)

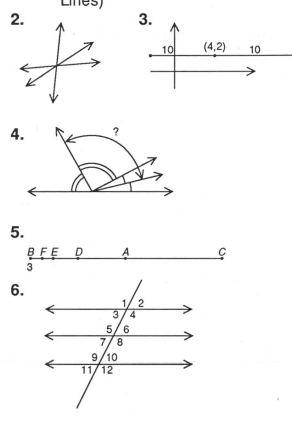

Page 37 (Geometry—Triangles)

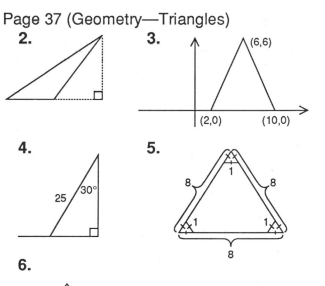

Page 38 (Geometry—Rectangles and Squares)

2.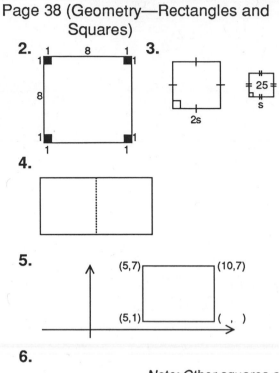

3.

4.

5.

6.

Note: Other squares are possible in the other three quadrants.

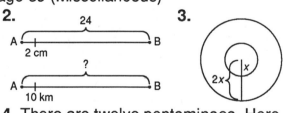

Page 39 (Miscellaneous)

2.

3.

4. There are twelve pentominoes. Here are some examples:

5.

6.

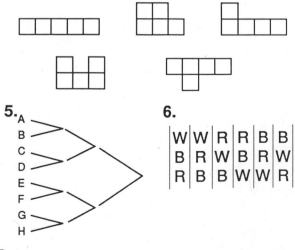

Page 40 (Miscellaneous)

2.

3. $(5 + 3)^2 \neq 5^2 + 3^2$ **4.**

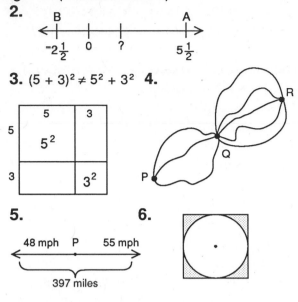

5.

48 mph   P   55 mph

397 miles

6.

Section 6: Dictionary Revisited

Page 43 (Analogies)
2. quart **3.** ordinal **4.** circumference
5. repeating decimal **6.** supplementary
7. cubic units **8.** cube **9.** 10 **10.** 3/8
11. obtuse **12.** 2.73×10^{-1}

Page 44 (Adjectives)
2. linear equation **3.** right triangle
4. similar polygons **5.** parallel lines
6. vertical angles **7.** obtuse angle
8. corresponding sides **9.** regular hexagon **10.** square root **11.** rectangular prism **12.** concentric circles

Page 45 (How Many?)
2. 4 **3.** 2 **4.** an infinite number **5.** 8
6. an infinite number **7.** 9 **8.** 7 **9.** 10
10. 9 **11.** 2 **12.** 64

Page 46 (What Comes Next?)
2. heptagon **3.** sevenths **4.** kilometer
5. ten thousandth **6.** L **7.** 32 **8.** 10,000
9. 1/81 **10.** 13 **11.** 25 **12.** 125

Page 47 (Opposites)
2. *Example:* 64; *Opposite:* square root; *Example:* 8   **3.** *Example:* 3; *Opposite:* composite; *Example:* 6   **4.** *Example:* a telephone pole; *Opposite:* horizontal; *Example:* a flat road

5. *Example:*

Opposite: parallel; *Example:* ─────────

6. *Example:*

A

Opposite: exterior; *Example:*

B

7. *Example:* 2 x 4 = 8; *Opposite:* half; *Example:* 2/2 = 1   **8.** *Example:* 45°; *Opposite:* obtuse; *Example:* 160°
9. *Example:* 2 + 2 = 4; *Opposite:* inequality; *Example:* 2 + 2 > 3
10. *Example:* 1 of 1/2; *Opposite:* denominator; *Example:* 2 of 1/2
11. *Example:* 1/5; *Opposite:* irrational; *Example:* π **12.** *Example:* .05; *Opposite:* repeating; *Example:* 0.333...

Page 48 (Insert a Word)
2. The cube of a <u>negative</u> number results in a negative number.   **3.** Every <u>nonzero</u> number has a reciprocal.   **4.** An altitude of <u>an obtuse</u> triangle falls outside the triangle.   **5.** The sum of <u>an even number of</u> odd numbers is even.   **6.** <u>An equilateral</u> triangle is equiangular.   **7.** Any median of <u>an equilateral</u> triangle is also an altitude.
8. A double of a <u>whole</u> number results in an even number.   **9.** The reciprocal of a <u>positive</u> number <u>less than one</u> is greater than the number.   **10.** The supplement of an <u>obtuse</u> angle will be an acute angle.
11. 5% <u>of $100.00</u> is exactly $5.00.
12. The nonparallel sides of <u>an isosceles</u> trapezoid are congruent.